Adventure in Alaska

An amazing true story of the world's longest, toughest dog sled race

by S. A. Kramer
with illustrations by Karen Meyer
and photographs

A Bullseye Nonfiction Book

Random House 🏠 New York

To Tracy and Duffer, and the years of joy

Based on *Race Across Alaska*, by Libby Riddles and Tim Jones. Grateful acknowledgement is made to the publisher, Stackpole Books of Mechanicsburg, Pennsylvania.

Cover design by Michaelis/Carpelis Design Associates, Inc.

Photos on pages 4 and 86 courtesy of AP/Wide World Photos
Photo on page 87 courtesy of Lew Tobin

Library of Congress Cataloging-in-Publication Data
Kramer, Sydelle.
Adventure in Alaska : an amazing true story of the world's longest, toughest dog sled race / by S.A. Kramer with illustrations by Karen Meyer and photographs.
    p. cm.
"A Read it to believe it! book."
SUMMARY: An account of Alaska's grueling, 1200-mile Iditarod dog sled race, won by a woman for the first time in 1985.
ISBN 0-679-84511-9 (pbk.). — ISBN 0-679-94511-3 (lib. bdg.)
1. Iditarod Trail Sled Dog Race, Alaska—Juvenile literature.
[1. Iditarod Trail Sled Dog Race, Alaska.   2. Sled dog racing.]
I. Meyer, Karen, ill.   II. Title.
SF440.15.K73 1993
798'.8—dc20 93-15753

Manufactured in the United States of America 10 9 8 7 6 5 4 3 2

Contents

Chapter 1

The Start

Libby Riddles is nervous. People are shouting all around her. Hundreds of dogs bark and whine and growl. Everywhere she looks, there are television cameras and reporters. It's so noisy and crowded, she can hardly think.

Today is March 2, 1985. Libby is in downtown Anchorage, Alaska. Soon she will start the world's longest, toughest race—the Iditarod Trail Sled Dog Race.

Libby is a musher, or a dog sled driver. The Iditarod is the most important race any musher can run. The finish line is close to twelve hun-

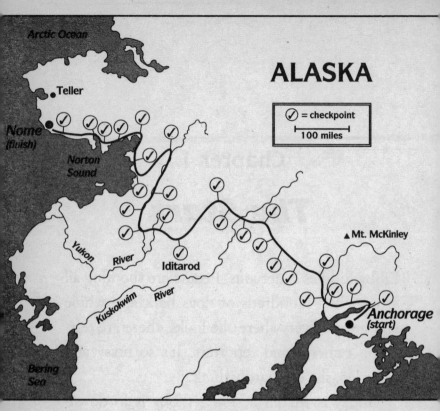

Mushers must stop at each checkpoint on the race route.

dred miles away. To reach it, she must cross
nearly all of Alaska. She'll speed from Anchorage
through wilderness the whole way to Nome. To
win, she must beat sixty other racers.

There's no road to follow, only a narrow trail

through deep snow. The trail plunges over mountains and shoots through thick forests. It tears down frozen rivers and crosses seas jammed with ice. It's full of steep, sharp turns that can make a sled crash.

At night, or in a storm, mushers can easily lose the trail. The sled can topple over or break any time. Libby and the dogs may have to fight through thirty-foot snowdrifts—high enough to bury trees.

The weather is unpredictable. A blizzard can hit when least expected. At night the temperature can sink to minus sixty degrees. It can get so cold, Libby's eyes could actually freeze in her head.

Then there's the wind. It can roar across the snow at eighty miles per hour. That's strong enough to blow her sled over and knock the dogs right off their feet.

Wolves, moose, and buffalo often prowl the trail. In past years they've menaced mushers, and killed or injured many dogs.

Libby knows all the risks. But she's not frightened—she's concentrating on doing her best. She and her fifteen dogs have trained long and hard for this day. Now practice is over—even the dogs know this is the real thing.

Twice before, Libby has run in the Iditarod and lost. Hardly anyone thinks she has a chance of winning this year. Many mushers are more experienced than she is. Some are racing with championship dogs. Besides, no woman has ever won the race.

Still, Libby thinks she could surprise everyone. She has faith in her dogs. They are stronger and faster than most people realize. She's raised them from pups and knows their families and their birthdays. She spends most of her time with them—they are her friends.

The dogs look like huskies, but they're a blend of three breeds—Alaskan malamute, Siberian husky, and the kind of sled dog Eskimos raise. Most have gray, brown, or black mixed with white in their coats. Dusty, though, is red, and Inca is all black. Stewpot, the biggest, looks part collie and part wolf.

The ugliest dog is Sister. She's the oldest on the team, too. She is nine years old, but still she always wants to fight. She's so mean she sometimes rips the ground up with her teeth. Her temper is so bad, she's torn her own dog house down. Now it's made of tin so she can't bite through it.

Yet Sister is very smart. Only Dugan is smarter. He often does what Libby wants before she can tell him. Sometimes she feels he knows exactly what she's thinking.

But Dugan is also stubborn. He'll sometimes decide on his own where to go. He especially likes to visit places he's already been. They may be totally out of the way, but Libby can't get him to change direction. Since the other dogs trust him, they follow his lead.

Now it's just a few minutes before Libby will take off. She moves toward the starting line. A red and yellow banner flies overhead. So many teams are racing that they can't start together. Each sled takes off separately every two minutes.

Libby's team will be the forty-sixth to go. She wears the number 46 over her parka. Forty-six is on the tags her dogs have on their collars. If

any of them get lost, that number will identify them.

Only two teams to go! The dogs are getting restless. They can hardly wait to race—they think they can win the Iditarod!

Libby checks the team quickly. All the dogs are harnessed up. Each harness is padded so it doesn't cut into their skin. It fits neatly around

the shoulders and body. A rope called the tug line connects the harness to the main rope. The main rope is called the tow or gang line.

So many ropes connect the sled and the team, the dogs can easily become tangled. Libby's always on guard so no dog gets choked.

She looks over the sled. Her food and equipment must be safe and secure. It's bundled tight on the sled, where the sides and back form a basket. The sled itself is long enough to sleep in.

It's almost time for the final countdown. Libby steps on the sled's runners. They look like skis and stretch out four feet behind the sled. To steady herself, she holds on to a bar in front of her.

Everything's ready! The countdown begins. "Ten, nine, eight," the official shouts. Libby takes a deep breath. Her long blond hair is tucked neatly under her fur hat. Her gloved hands grip the bar of the sled firmly.

"Seven, six, five, four." The dogs strain

against their harnesses. Libby is as excited as they are. For so many years, she's dreamed of winning the Iditarod. Now she's ready to race, day or night, snow or sun.

"Three, two, one!"

"Mush!" Libby shouts. The dogs leap forward. The race is on!

Chapter 2

The First Day

Libby and the team charge down the streets of Anchorage. The dogs are running so fast, she is worried. Sleds often crash on the sharp turns around street corners. Some mushers never make it out of the city.

She yells out the commands her dogs learned as puppies—"mush!" means let's go and "whoa!" means stop, "gee" means go right and "haw" means turn left. To steer, she stands up straight or leans one way or the other.

After just a few blocks, Libby and the team

start to feel hot. It's about twenty-five degrees, but that's too warm for them. Some mushers feel it's best to race at minus twenty degrees. Then the dogs don't overheat or get as tired.

To make sure the weather is cold enough, Libby plans to race at night. In order to see in the dark, she'll wear a special light called a head-lamp. It cuts through the gloom like the head-lights of a car.

Racing at night means Libby won't get much sleep. But other mushers do it too—they think it's the only way to win.

Soon Libby and the team leave the city streets behind. The sun is bright as they speed along. It's easy to find the trail when the weather is good. Snowmobiles have cut a path, and stakes called markers are in the ground to help show the way.

Libby spots a group of trees with hardly any space between them. The trail curves around, but the dogs aim right for the trees. They're so excited they don't listen to her commands. Libby can't see a way through—the sled is sure to crash!

The Iditarod has just begun, and already she's in trouble. It's dark among the trees. The sled slams off trunk after trunk. She holds on tight, and keeps her feet on the runners.

Suddenly there's daylight. They burst into open space! Somehow they've made it through, and the sled's still in one piece.

The trail is so straight now, she can see the whole team in front of her. Dugan and Bugs are running almost forty feet ahead. Today they are the lead dogs. Their job is to spot the trail and keep the team on it. They must obey Libby's commands, and pick the right speed to travel.

Right behind Dugan and Bugs are Inca and Binga. Today they're what's called the swing dogs—they help steer the sled.

Ten other dogs—the team dogs—follow. Axle

is with Dusty, and Sister is with Penny. Tip and Minnow run together. So do Stripe and Socks. After them come Whitey and Brownie. Team dogs run in pairs and don't steer or find the trail. Their job is hard enough—they pull the sled.

Stewpot comes last. He is the wheel dog. Wheel dogs must be strong, fast, and steady. Since he's closest to the sled, Stewpot pulls its weight first. With the runners just behind him, he must be quick and stay out of their way. The sled makes a lot of noise slashing through the snow—Stewpot can't ever let it bother him.

Libby will shift many of the dogs around later. They like to do different jobs so they don't get bored. Most of the time the lead dog will be Dugan. Sister will get an easier job so she doesn't get tired out. Libby wants to keep her healthy in case there's an emergency.

The team is running smoothly. Libby is pleased with their pace. Dusty moves surprisingly fast despite his wide body. Socks may be

small, but she's really strong. Stripe is a rookie but easily keeps up with the others.

In the team's middle, Tip and Minnow speed along happily. They're sisters, and Libby can barely tell them apart. But Tip's coat is cleaner—she always licks it till it shines. Minnow's tail is a lot curlier. If one of them wanders off, it's always Tip—Minnow is more obedient than her sister.

Libby relaxes as the sled glides along. Then

suddenly, Dugan and Bugs leap into the air. Inca and Binga jump too, and then Axle and Dusty. There's something up ahead, and it's blocking the trail! The dogs can bound over it, but the sled will hit it head on.

Smack! The sled topples over. Libby flies off the runners. But she manages to keep her hands on the steering bar. She can hardly believe her eyes when she sees what she's slammed into. It's an old washing machine, and it's sticking out of the ice. Someone living nearby must have dumped it long ago. Now it might keep her from winning the Iditarod.

The dogs keep going, and somehow Libby hangs on to the sled. With a few quick moves, she tips it back on its runners. She can't believe her luck has been this bad. Two narrow escapes, and she's just been racing for an hour.

In the afternoon, the team reaches a special stopping place called a checkpoint. Twenty-five checkpoints are scattered along the trail. Some are villages, others are just cabins or tents. There, mushers rest and eat, and take care of their teams. They also pick up new supplies.

No sled can carry everything a musher needs—it would be too heavy for the dogs to pull. So before the race starts, mushers ship food and extra equipment to the checkpoints.

As other mushers move around her, Libby unharnesses the dogs. It's the warmest part of the day, and they quickly lap up fresh water. They bite and swallow snow to cool themselves off. Soon Whitey lies down—she works hard yet loves to rest. But Minnow, Bugs, and Tip roll on their backs in the drifts.

A race official checks the supplies on Libby's sled. There are always officials at the checkpoints. Iditarod rules say mushers must carry certain equipment. If Libby doesn't have everything, she will be disqualified.

She has snowshoes to cross deep drifts, and an arctic sleeping bag for icy weather. She needs an axe to chop up firewood, ice, and frozen food.

Her sled must carry two pounds of food per dog, plus a day's worth for herself. To prepare hot meals, she must pack a cooker, or small stove. Libby tries to feed the dogs a hot meal every sixty miles.

She must also bring special socks called booties for the dogs. They wear them when the trail is rough or icy. Booties protect their feet from cuts and bruises. They keep ice from scraping the pads on their paws raw, and snow from bunching up in between the toes. A musher must pack eight booties per dog. A team can use as many as a thousand during the Iditarod.

But sometimes booties can't prevent an injury. A dog with a hurt paw won't be able to run. The dog will be left at the next checkpoint and dropped from the race.

The team waits anxiously to start running again. They've traveled less than one hundred miles and still have energy to burn. Suddenly Sister loses her patience—she jumps straight into the air. All four paws leave the ground again and again. She leaps up and down as if she were a bouncing ball.

Unlike Sister, Penny waits calmly. She's such a good dog, Libby sometimes forgets she's there. Penny is sweet and fast and steady. She never causes problems for Libby.

At last Libby's ready to go. A big crowd cheers as she leaves. For miles the dogs speed up the trail—but suddenly it splits in two. There's no way of telling which way to turn. Libby steers the team up one path—but there are no sled tracks on it. Now she knows they're heading in the wrong direction!

Libby hates having to turn the sled around. It takes up a lot of time, and the ropes usually end up all tangled. Axle, who's clumsy, often gets twisted up in them. Sure enough, as Libby watches, the ropes knot and curl.

Then a dog starts barking. The others join in. One of the team is in trouble. It's not Axle—it's Minnow! A rope is wound tight around her neck.

Libby leaps from the sled. The dogs are jumping and whining. Only Minnow is silent—she is choking.

The rope gets tighter and tighter. Minnow looks frightened. At last Libby reaches her and quickly untangles her. Minnow wags her crooked tail—she knows Libby has saved her.

They race until eight that night. Then Libby decides it's time for a rest. She does not want the team to be too tired tomorrow.

She ties the sled to a small spruce tree just off the trail. But the dogs don't want to nap—they're still too excited. Inca barks as if she's saying, Let's keep moving.

Two teams go by, and Sister begins whining. She tries to chase the passing dogs. She and Dugan leap about, all four feet in the air. Even Brownie, who's usually calm, is very restless.

Soon the whole team is yapping. They pull and pull against the tree. Suddenly Libby hears a thud—they've yanked the tree over! It's fallen to the side, but it's still in the ground.

She has no choice but to leave now. The dogs may hurt themselves tugging. Teams this worked up don't stop until they're free. Even roped to a pickup truck, they'll just drag it down a trail.

But she can't untie the sled. The rope has been pulled much too tight. Libby can't cut the rope—she's going to need it later. The only way to free the sled is to chop through the tree.

Libby grabs her axe and gives the tree one sharp whack after another. It doesn't budge. Then the dogs tug furiously. Snap! The tree cracks! The team takes off like a stampeding herd.

They're running away! Libby doesn't know what to do. First the sled whips by her, and then the rope and the tree. She sticks out her hand and grabs on to the wood. But it's moving so fast she's knocked right off her feet.

"Whoa!" she yells out, but none of the dogs listen. They haul her along on her belly through deep snow. Her arms are so strong, she hangs on for two miles. But finally she has to let go.

Still, she doesn't give up. She bolts full speed after the team. But they easily outrun her. Soon they're out of sight.

She keeps running anyway. Somehow she has to find the dogs. Just when she's too tired to go

on, another musher rides out of the night. He puts her on his sled and starts searching for the team. It's an Iditarod custom for drivers to help each other. A good-sportsmanship prize is awarded at the end of the race.

There's no sign of the dogs. The musher's headlamp sweeps through the dark. Suddenly Libby spots wild eyes reflecting the light. It's her team straight ahead. She can't believe her luck!

Another musher has stopped them and tied them to some trees.

Libby runs over. She tries to act angry. But the dogs aren't injured, and she's so happy to see them. They're resting quietly—they don't think they've done anything wrong. Libby thanks the musher again and again.

She's got her team back—she can still win this race.

Chapter 3

On the Trail

It's two in the morning at the next checkpoint, about a hundred miles into the race. Libby is wide awake—she's just heard a terrible story. A moose on the trail has attacked a musher and her team. The musher is injured, and two of her dogs are dead. She has had to drop out of the race.

Libby is worried. Moose often appear on this part of the trail. They can weigh sixteen hundred pounds, and be very stubborn. A train may be steaming toward them, but they won't budge from the tracks. They'll kick and stomp their way through a dog team if the team frightens them.

The dogs can't escape—they get tangled in their ropes.

Everyone at the checkpoint is talking about the moose. But Libby tries to ignore them—she has to start her chores. There are certain jobs she must do at every checkpoint. The faster she works, the quicker she'll be back on the trail.

First, she looks for the food that she's shipped here. She's spray-painted the bags purple and green so they're easy to spot.

Then she fetches water for herself and the team. Here there are no faucets or fountains. Libby walks across a frozen lake to a hole chopped in the ice. She dips her bucket in and lugs the water back. As hard as this is, it's easier than melting snow.

As soon as her fire is ready, she starts the team's meal. All the dog food has frozen because it's so cold. She takes her axe and chops the food into bits. Then she dumps the bits into a pot of boiling water.

Libby isn't cooking regular dog food. Iditarod dogs eat beef and liver, chicken, lamb, and fish. The food is specially prepared by each musher. Then it is mixed with dry dog food and water.

Libby puts extra water in the food to prevent what's called dehydration. Cold weather makes dogs and people very thirsty. Just like heat, cold dries their bodies out. When that happens, they get weak, sick, and dizzy. Along with food, Libby gulps down bottles of juice. That way she won't get dehydrated.

When the dogs have eaten, she gathers her trash. She must bring it to a special garbage dump at each checkpoint.

There's no time to sleep. She has to be on her way quickly. Later, she and the team will be required to rest. Iditarod rules don't allow the dogs to get too exhausted.

Back on the trail, the snow is soft and deep. Libby stops often to pry ice balls off the dogs' paws. Sometimes she puts ointment on them to ease the pain from sores. The ointment also helps any cuts heal faster. Occasionally she rubs their shoulders so their muscles won't ache.

She tries different dogs in the lead with Dugan. Bugs loves to be up front but doesn't always concentrate on where he's going. Libby calls him an "airbrain" and a "turkey." When Brownie takes over, he mixes up commands. Dusty sulks if she corrects him.

She could pair Sister with Dugan, but he's a little afraid of her. Besides, Libby wants to save Sister in case of trouble. She knows she can count on her in a storm. Nothing frightens Sister.

It's less than twenty-four hours since the race began. But Libby is already tired. At times she falls asleep standing on the sled. To keep awake, she plugs her Walkman in. Rock 'n' roll music blasts straight into her ears. There's no one to hear her so she sings out loud.

At last it's dawn. Libby spots a strange object

ahead. It's standing absolutely still in the middle of the trail. As the morning light grows brighter, she watches it closely. Her bad luck may not have run out.

The dogs' ears go forward. They raise their heads and slow down. A moose is blocking the trail! Its head is down, its face is fierce. Libby can

tell it's not going to budge.

She has to try to go around it. But will the team listen to her commands? The dogs love to chase animals, Dusty especially.

"Gee," Libby orders. All the dogs obey. This moose looks too dangerous to approach. They make a wide loop around it and head on their way.

Later, Libby hears another musher wasn't so lucky. The moose charged over and knocked her off her sled. Then it stood right over her for twenty minutes. But it finally walked away without hurting her or her dogs.

Finally it's time to rest. The dogs dig shallow holes in the snow to sleep. They pack the snow down and curl up inside. If it's very cold, they put their tails over their noses.

Libby tries to rest too. She must keep up her strength. It's only the second day of the race, but she can't stop worrying. If she falls too far behind the leaders, she may never catch up. She only has time to sleep a couple of hours each day.

Soon she's ready to go. Now they're traveling through real wilderness. They streak through deep forests, and up and down mountains. Libby often runs beside the sled and helps the dogs by pushing. They pad through the snow and the sled swishes behind them. She watches the team run—racing seems to make them happy. They are also eager to please Libby.

She understands that they need praise, and encouragement, too. She talks to them often, and tells them what good dogs they are. Tip and Whitey shake with delight whenever Libby pets them. Bug-eyed Axle gets embarrassed, but Penny is pleased. Brownie and Dugan don't seem to care.

The trail soon leads to the edge of a deep canyon. A canyon is a narrow valley between two cliffs. At the bottom of the canyon is the frozen Happy River. Libby is so far above it, it looks like a silver thread.

Suddenly the trail disappears over the side. The drop is so steep, it's almost like a carnival slide. Libby remembers that this is one of the most dangerous spots in the Iditarod.

The sled shoots down the cliff. The trail zigs and zags. Libby brakes hard but the dogs are flying. The sled tips on one side and then another. It skids into a snowbank, then somersaults through the air!

Somehow Libby holds on. She's not hurt when she lands. She's come down in deep snow up to her armpits. But if the team keeps running, she'll be dragged down the cliff.

"Stay!" she cries out—and the dogs listen. She hauls the sled out of the snow and somehow turns it over. "Go ahead, easy, easy," she says to them all. They seem to realize the danger and obey without question.

At last they reach the bottom. Libby stops for a rest and gives out snacks. Every hour or so the team gets hunks of frozen meat or fish. These snacks give the dogs the energy to keep racing. Their favorite is the whitefish she's prepared herself. She rolls it up so when it freezes, it looks like a Popsicle.

Libby needs energy too. She gets most of it from eating junk food. She knows that's not healthy, but often when she's racing, it's all she can eat. She's packed pizza and popcorn and Kentucky Fried Chicken. She's got frozen yogurt, pecan pie, and peanut butter sandwiches.

But one of her favorite treats is kamamik, or Eskimo ice cream. Kamamik is made of salmonberries, reindeer fat, seal oil, and sugar. Libby's kamamik was made by an Eskimo woman from her hometown.

After the snacks, they're on their way. The sky begins to darken—there's a storm coming up. Can they reach the next checkpoint before it snows? The team races the weather, but Socks and Stewpot seem tired. Libby notices their ears are back. Something may be wrong.

Socks is the team's smallest dog, but she's very strong. Stewpot is big and hardly ever seems to weaken. Now both dogs are moving slowly and have diarrhea. They've caught a virus and may spread it to the others.

Just before the storm hits, Libby makes it to the checkpoint. The veterinarian there gives Socks and Stewpot medicine. If they don't get better soon, Libby will have to leave them behind.

She sits next to them in the snow, petting and soothing them. She hates to see them both suffering. "How's old Stewbones?" she says. "And you there, Socks. How's my girl?" She gives them special snacks to try to get them to eat. But poor Stewpot, who usually stuffs himself, won't touch a thing.

The storm is bad. Two feet of snow falls in the mountains. Planes can't fly into the next checkpoint with food and supplies. For the first time ever, the Iditarod is delayed. Only three days old, the race is stopped until the planes can get through.

No matter how cold it is, the team must sleep outside. To keep the dogs warm, Libby gathers spruce tree branches. She makes each a soft bed and takes their harnesses off. They curl up and sleep on the branches for hours.

But when anyone walks by, they jump to their feet. The whole team growls and barks—they're protecting Libby from strangers. After a while, no one will come near them. They're so ferocious one official calls them "alligators."

Three nights go by before the race starts again. Libby's almost out of food—she can't wait to get to the next checkpoint. But the rest has done Socks and Stewpot a lot of good. They both seem healthy again.

The wind is cold but the sky is clear. Inca barks sharply. Bugs is anxious to move. Off the team goes, straight into the wind.

Soon huge drifts have whisked over the trail.

Some of the markers are totally buried. It seems impossible to Libby that a path was ever there.

She tries to concentrate. She studies the land ahead. Then her heart starts to pound. She has no idea where she is!

Her best guess is to go straight ahead. But Dugan turns to the right. He seems to think he knows better than Libby. The more he refuses to listen, the madder she gets.

He keeps cutting to the right, his strong legs kicking up snow. Libby has had enough—she is about to stop the team and tell Dugan off. But all of a sudden she sees the trail in front of her! Dugan has somehow sensed it all along. The dogs were never lost. Only she was.

Libby jumps from the sled and makes her way to Dugan. She kneels in front of him and looks into his blue eyes. Then she scratches his ears and tells him she's sorry. He just shakes himself off—he wants to keep racing.

Libby understands that she has a lot to learn

from her team. The dogs give her their all, and expect so little back. As they happily speed on, she feels full of love for them. Even if they don't win the Iditarod, they are true champions.

Chapter 4

Chasing the Leaders

It is the sixth day of the race. Libby and the team have covered close to two hundred fifty miles. The sun is setting as Dugan and Axle lead the dogs into a canyon called Hell's Gate. Penny's ears shoot up. Inca and Bugs sniff the air. Even Sister seems a little nervous.

Suddenly there's a howl. The dogs stop in their tracks. A second howl rings out. The dogs don't make a sound. Libby sees them all staring in the same direction. Something is wrong—the fur on their backs is rising.

The howling continues. It's two wolves calling. The dogs are motionless. Libby wonders if the wolves are sending messages to each other.

For ten minutes, the dogs are as still as snowmen. Then they take off. Fear is in their eyes. They keep turning their heads to make sure no wolf is following.

The howls echo through the canyon. Libby feels like the only person on earth. There's just the mountains, the icy river, and the wolves.

Through the woods they speed. Dugan and Axle are in the lead. They are brothers and make a good team. They're both well behaved and run stride for stride. But while Axle is friendlier, Dugan is wiser. Somehow Axle senses this and wants to learn.

They zoom onto a frozen river. Libby's in a hurry—she wants to move closer to the lead. She knows there are other sleds in front of her.

Suddenly she sees her axe hanging out of the sled. The bag that holds all her supplies has a big rip in it. She knows she must stop and sew the bag up right away. If anything gets lost, it could cost her the race.

She finds a needle in her equipment. There's no thread, but she does have a spool of mint-flavored dental floss. She quickly rips some off and sticks it through the needle. With just a few stitches, she patches the bag.

Behind her soar blue mountains. Ahead, the earth looks dead. Fallen trees black as coal lie slumped on their sides. Jagged stumps poke their edges up through the snow. Everywhere she looks, there are the scars of a great fire.

Libby has reached a place called the Farewell Burn. A few years before, Alaska's biggest forest fire tore through here.

The Burn can be dangerous for a musher. A hidden stump can destroy a sled. Wandering buffalo will sometimes attack a team. A wind is always roaring, and the sun reflects harshly off the snow. Libby puts on special goggles to protect her eyes.

The dogs have no problems with the Burn. They whiz right through it. The team is making good time—then bad luck strikes again. Bugs, Binga, and Inca begin to feel sick. While the others wolf down their snacks, those three won't eat.

Usually Bugs is fidgety, but now he doesn't want to move. Binga's big brown eyes tell Libby he feels miserable. Inca seems the worst. For the first time ever, she doesn't want to play.

Libby puts her on the sled. She scratches her ears. Inca loves attention, but now she's too sick to care. She eats some Kentucky Fried Chicken. Then she lays her black-and-white muzzle on Libby's leg.

Libby is upset. She needs Inca on the team. Of all the dogs, she's the most loyal—she comes whenever she's called. Besides, she's Libby's favorite. She was born on Libby's birthday. She always jumps up and throws herself all over Libby. When they play together, Inca barks and clicks her teeth.

Libby needs Bugs and Binga too. Bugs loves to race. Each time he's harnessed, he trembles with excitement. He often rolls on his back and barks at the team. Binga, his brother, is quiet but

just as strong. He loves to run too.

The team races on despite the sick dogs. It starts to snow. Soon the flakes are falling so fast and thick, the trail markers begin to vanish. Frost coats Libby's hair.

Suddenly the dogs begin to disappear! One by one they drop out of sight. The trail has

stumbled down into a half-frozen creek. The team splashes through—but the sled gets stuck. Libby must wade through the water in order to free it.

The dogs are all wet. Libby keeps an eye on Dugan. She knows he hates it when his whiskers get soaked. But he and the other dogs just shake the water off. Then they roll in the snow to help their fur dry.

The team is fine—but Libby's not sure she is. One of her boots has leaked, and her foot is dripping. She quickly changes her sock, but there's nothing else she can do. Libby's worried. Getting wet and cold can make a person's temperature fall below normal. This condition is called hypothermia.

Hypothermia keeps the brain from doing its job. Blood stops flowing to both the fingers and toes. Most of the muscles have trouble moving. In the Iditarod it gets so cold that sweating alone can cause hypothermia.

Luckily for Libby, it's not too chilly. She hurries on to the next checkpoint—a village called Nikolai. Although it's one-thirty in the morning in the middle of a snowstorm, children are outside waiting for autographs. To them, the Iditarod is more important than the Super Bowl.

Libby discovers the race is close. She's only three and a half hours behind the leader. She wants to catch up, so she sleeps for only an hour. While she's napping, someone dries her boot with a hair dryer.

On the trail again, Libby travels slowly. The snow has stopped, but Bugs, Binga, and Inca still won't eat. Brownie's sick too—he rolls his soft brown eyes at her. Will she lose four dogs to illness and have to drop them from the race?

Iditarod rules say a team can be as small as seven dogs, or as big as twenty. But the fewer dogs a musher has, the more tired each dog gets. It will be hard for Libby to win if she has to run with only eleven dogs.

She stops for a rest and takes off her fur hat. When her long hair tumbles down, she decides to try and brush it. It hasn't been combed since the race started over a week ago. Now it's so tangled up, the brush breaks in her hand.

She feels filthy. If only she could change her clothes. But she didn't pack any extras—there's no room on the sled. A bath would be even better, but there are no tubs out here. There's just snow wherever she looks, and a frozen river among the trees.

At the next checkpoint she tells the dogs what a good job they're doing. From her voice, the dogs know she's very proud of them. Libby believes praising the dogs makes them a stronger team.

She plays with Tip and Minnow, and watches Dusty do his backflips. She gently strokes Penny, who scrunches up her face. Whispering in his ear, she tells blue-eyed Axle he's handsome. She even pets Brownie, who doesn't always like her.

Libby knows the dogs can sense her mood. If she's depressed, they get depressed, too. So no matter how tired she is, or how discouraged, she tries to be in good spirits when she's with the team.

At night, the dogs get a special treat. Libby makes beds out of straw for each one of them. But while the others go right to sleep, Sister isn't satisfied. She digs a little hole and arranges the straw herself.

Whitey, Sister's daughter, isn't as fussy as her mother. She only wants to sleep, and curls right up. But Stripe, Sister's son, watches his mother carefully. He copies her exactly.

Libby gets a treat too. She sleeps in a real bed. There's also a bathroom she can use, with steaming hot water. Her own home in Alaska has no indoor plumbing. There's no running water—not even a shower. The toilet is outside.

Libby's house is a cabin in a small town called Teller. Only two hundred fifty people live there, most of them Eskimo. Teller is a long way from Wisconsin, where Libby grew up. Her father was a college professor, and her family led a comfortable life.

But Libby never cared about comfort. She wanted adventure. So she left Wisconsin at the age of sixteen. She worked her way across America and finally reached Alaska. When she heard about the Iditarod, she knew she'd found what she wanted to do.

Now she's twenty-nine years old, and owns thirty sled dogs. She trains with them all year, and also works different jobs. She's done everything from making hats to packing Pepsi bottles.

Her life isn't easy. She doesn't earn much money. But Libby has no regrets. When she's racing in the Iditarod, anything seems possible.

Right now she's so tired, all she wants to do is rest. The bed is so soft. The heated house is so warm. But nothing's more important to her than winning this race.

An hour passes. Then she makes herself get up and leave. She tells herself over and over, "Plenty of time to sleep later."

The night air is freezing. Her breath turns into puffs of smoke. Bugs and Binga, Inca and Brownie are still sick, but run hard.

Nine teams race in the distance ahead of her. Will she be able to catch them? Into the darkness her dogs fly.

Chapter 5

Closing the Gap

More than a week has gone by since the Iditarod started. All Libby can think about is how exhausted she is. As the sled speeds along, she tries hard not to fall asleep. She sings songs to the dogs to keep herself awake.

When mushers get weary and are alone on the trail, they sometimes see and hear things that aren't really there. This is called hallucinating. Once, in a past race, Libby imagined a sled was in her way. Now she begins to think tree branches block the trail. She tries to swat them away—but she's only beating air.

In the fresh wet snow, the sled feels very heavy. She seems to be creeping along when another team comes up behind her. Soon there are others. They want to pass. It's an Iditarod rule that Libby must pull off the trail. No one is allowed to slow down another musher.

She feels discouraged watching the sleds slide past. Bugs and Stripe bark and howl at the dogs racing by. Her team is losing ground—are the sick dogs slowing her down?

Ahead, there are rolling hills. The sled crawls up, then glides down. Suddenly Brownie pulls to the side and grabs something off the ground. One of the mushers has dropped a piece of frozen meat. Brownie gobbles it up—he must be feeling better!

At the next checkpoint, she learns that the race has been stopped again. There's a bad storm ahead, and planes can't get through to drop food.

Libby is relieved—she and the team will get a rest. The three sick dogs will have time to get better.

She settles the dogs in for a long stay. First she unharnesses them, then ties them to some trees. Even though he's sick, Bugs snaps at the others. He makes what Libby calls "horrible faces." She grabs him and ties him to his own tree.

Then Stewpot and Stripe start barking at one another. Stripe is often grouchy and attacks any dog that's too close. Libby ties them up separately to prevent a fight. But Stripe keeps growling and tries to pull the tree down.

Whitey is desperate to get out of the way. Whenever there's an argument, she tries to disappear.

Socks gets her own tree too. Libby can't tie her to the main rope. She might chomp right through it, since she loves to chew rope. If the gang line snaps, all the dogs will run free. Libby outsmarts Socks—she uses a chain to tie her up.

Then Libby gathers up everything that's wet. The dogs' booties and harnesses are always drenched. So are her clothes, from both snow and sweat. At each checkpoint, she hangs them by a fire to dry. If she can't dry her parka, she turns it inside out in the cold. In a little while the moisture freezes and she scrapes it off like frost.

A day and a half passes. Then the race starts up once again. All the mushers are anxious. They know there's no more time to waste. Whoever takes the lead now has the best chance to win the Iditarod.

Libby gets ready. The dogs seem to know they must move fast. Binga feels better—he's drooling with excitement. Axle is so eager he practically harnesses himself.

The sled glides out smoothly. Libby feels relaxed. The beam of her headlamp shoots far into the night. The miles roll past—then suddenly the dogs rocket forward. The sled whips around curves like a roller coaster.

The team is out of control. Libby hits the brake. She screams at the dogs to stop. But they ignore her. It's as though she weren't there.

The dogs are chasing caribou, a type of reindeer. Libby's heart is hammering. Will the sled get smashed? Will the team get exhausted and be unable to go on?

Luckily the dogs never leave the trail. For five miles, they careen along at top speed.

Finally, the hunt is over. The dogs slow to a trot. It's not that they're tired—they can't smell the caribou anymore.

Soon, the sun comes up over gently rolling land. Nothing blocks Libby's view—it's as though she can see forever. As tiny as she is on this great stretch of earth, she feels she belongs here—she's a part of all she sees.

The dogs rush on as though they'll never get

tired. Bugs, Binga, and Inca run as fast as the others—Libby is relieved that they're healthy again. They come to the town of Iditarod, the halfway point in the race. The first musher here wins two thousand dollars in silver coins. Libby is fourth, but she's still pleased. The team has gained a lot of ground, and they're close to the lead.

Iditarod is now a ghost town. But it was booming in 1908, when gold was discovered nearby. Local Indians gave the town its name—Iditarod means "the distant place."

Back then, dog sleds were the only transportation. All supplies—even the mail—were hauled by dogs. The sled trail ran all the way to Nome, the nearest big city.

Then in 1925, a deadly disease called diphtheria struck Nome. It threatened to wipe out the whole population. Medicine to treat it was stored twelve hundred miles away in Anchorage. Somehow, in the dead of winter, the medicine had to get to Nome.

But the sea was frozen, so ships couldn't sail. Airplanes in those days couldn't fly through snow and ice. A train could carry the medicine— but the tracks stopped 674 miles from Nome. From there, the Iditarod trail was the only road.

Twenty mushers volunteered to carry the medicine. They set up a relay team to dash from the train to Nome. The dogs had to fight through blizzard after blizzard. Eighty-mile-an-hour winds screamed across the ice. The temperature rarely rose above minus thirty.

Yet the medicine reached Nome in time to save the city. The dogs and the mushers had out-raced death. In 1973, to honor their achievement, the Iditarod Trail Sled Dog Race was begun.

As Libby leaves Iditarod, another storm hits. It's close to impossible to see any trail markers. Parts of the trail lie buried under four feet of snow.

Two teams are right behind her. One is ahead.

The lead keeps changing hands all during the night. Her dogs struggle on through the dark and deep snow. She feels like they've been racing forever, but there's no time for a break.

Ahead the trail is smooth. The snow lies unbroken. It seems as if no one in the world has ever been here before. Suddenly she realizes why there are no tracks to follow. She's the first musher to come through. She's in first place!

Chapter 6

Taking a Risk

Through the woods they sprint. There's still over five hundred miles to go. But despite the dark, Dugan easily finds the trail. Libby doesn't have to worry with him in the lead. She knows he runs even better when she's not giving him orders.

Libby feels exhausted. The swish of the sled is like a lullaby. She tries to stay awake, but it gets harder and harder. Balanced on the runners, she drops off to sleep.

Bam! She hits a tree branch! It bashes her right in the head. Her headlamp cuts out, then smacks her on the nose. Blood drips down her face as total darkness surrounds her.

The first thing Libby does is check the lamp. If it's broken, she won't be able to keep racing. But it switches right back on, and the dogs speed ahead. Her nose is sore, but she's grateful it's not broken.

At the next checkpoint, she sleeps for two hours. Now her lead is gone—other teams have passed her. But she's more worried about Stewpot. His tongue is hanging out. He's not hunting for little animals the way he usually does. Instead, as they take off, he bends to grab mouthfuls of snow. If Stewpot is sick again, the team is in trouble.

Something's wrong with Stripe, too. His paws are sore and swollen. He hates to wear booties, and keeps trying to shake them off. If his paws don't improve, Stripe will have to be left behind.

They zoom across the tundra, a flat land. It can get so boring that dogs fall asleep while they run. Dugan and Axle are getting along well in the lead. Axle's a good follower, and he lets Dugan feel in charge.

The tundra leads them to the Yukon River. It's frozen solid and a mile wide. They have to race down the river for one hundred fifty miles. The temperature plunges. Winds can be sixty miles an hour.

Libby has been racing for twelve days and she has never felt so cold. Not even four layers of clothing can keep her warm. Her fur hat and hood protect her head, but her arms, legs, and feet feel like ice. She runs beside the sled to keep her blood flowing. To prevent frostbite, she pumps her arms and kicks her feet.

Libby is afraid of frostbite. She knows it can strike at these temperatures. Her skin will freeze like water, turning hard and white. She won't have any feeling in places where she's frostbitten. Worse, fingers and toes can turn black and actually break off.

The dogs aren't cold at all. They run like

they'll never get tired. And Stewpot is back to normal. Libby realizes the weather was too hot for him. "That's the way, Stewbones," she calls out. Stewpot seems to smile back at her.

In the gleam of her headlamp, the dogs look "like ghosts." Frost shines off their coats, and their breath spreads out like fog.

The night is pure black. The sky is jammed with stars. Suddenly Libby sees ribbons of radiant colors far above her. They flash across the sky

like streamers at a party. Green, yellow, and red, they're called the northern lights. In their glow, the snow turns pink all around her. It's so beautiful that Libby forgets how chilly she is.

But the wind keeps stabbing through her. It's forty degrees below zero. She thinks about Hawaii to try to warm up. Nothing helps, though. All she can do is keep moving.

The hours pass. By the next night, the weather gets even colder. Libby puts on an extra pair of pants. She also pulls on her mukluks— boots made of sealskin and reindeer fur.

Next comes a special jacket called a pullover parka. She made it herself from lambskin and wolf fur. It has no buttons or zippers for the wind to lash through.

But she's still freezing, and can hardly move. The frigid air seems to be in her blood. The temperature has fallen to fifty-two degrees below zero.

It's too cold to rest, but Libby stops the dogs

anyway. Their booties must be changed so the ice can't cut into their paws. She peels off her gloves and uses her bare hands. To keep her fingers from turning numb, she warms them on the dogs.

The whole team is frisky, although it's cold enough to crack steel. Stripe is feeling better—he barks to go on. But Libby can't stop shivering. A night like this can freeze a deer in its tracks. Mushers have passed them standing dead, eyes iced open in shock.

She wraps her sleeping bag around her. Once she's warmer, exhaustion hits. As the dogs race on, she begins to hallucinate. Branches seem to be flying at her head. She ducks so she won't get hit—but there's nothing there.

They head toward the Bering Sea, past check-point after checkpoint. To the dogs, Libby thinks, running is as easy as breathing. Yet as the sun warms the air, Stripe looks more and more unhappy. He puts his ears back and begins to slow down. Libby decides his paws are hurting. Now she'll have to drop him from the race, or he may limp for the rest of his life. When he reaches a town, he'll be flown home to Teller, for some time off. Then he'll be ready to race again.

Libby is proud of Stripe. He's almost as tough as his mother. This is only his first race, but he's lasted fifteen days.

At the next checkpoint, Libby unloads supplies from her sled. It's important to make it as light as possible. With only 269 miles to Nome, speed will determine the winner. Libby has arrived here in second place. She wants to take over first.

Other mushers have been dumping supplies along the trail. They've gotten rid of gloves and socks, stoves and underwear—anything they don't think they need anymore. Libby grabs booties whenever she sees them. She has a feeling they'll be useful before the race is over.

Less than three hundred miles to go. They

leave the checkpoint before anyone else. The sun is so bright even Sister's dirty white coat shines. Libby heads through the hills and comes out on flat land. The wind is strong enough to shove snow through her zipper.

She puts on her sealskin mittens and her pullover parka. Is the weather bad enough to put Sister in the lead? Axle and Dugan don't seem to mind the wind slapping their faces. The day might get worse—she'll save Sister for then.

A storm is raging by the time they reach the next checkpoint. Snow is piling onto drifts already higher than houses. The fierce wind never stops—it may cause what mushers call a whiteout. Swirling flakes will hide everything from sight.

For the next sixty miles, Libby knows the wind will drive right at them. Snow will sting their faces. Frost will cling to their hair. The temperature might dive even lower than before.

Even worse, forty miles of the trail will be on

sea ice. And in a blinding storm, it will be impossible to see where the ice is broken. The team could slip through a crack and plunge straight into the water. If they don't all drown, hypothermia will kill them.

Should she go on? The mushers who are just arriving say it's too dangerous to continue. They will stay at the checkpoint until the storm is over.

Libby knows first place is at stake. If she leaves now, she'll have a head start over everyone. But she'll also be taking a tremendous risk. She could get lost and freeze to death.

The wind is now seventy miles per hour. The temperature is dropping below zero and there's still daylight. With one part of her mind, Libby thinks, "You fool, this is crazy." Then the other part says, "You must. You must try for this. This is the most important thing in your life."

Darkness is approaching as she prepares a new, lighter sled she has waiting. Despite the wind and cold, she puts booties on all the dogs.

Another musher approaches her and says, "What are you doing?…It's impossible."

His words make Libby more determined than ever. Moments later, she leaves the checkpoint. She can hardly see the snowmobile leading her to the trail. In the howling wind, she feels a little afraid. Will she regret her decision?

The dogs bend their heads and push into the north wind.

Chapter 7

The Blizzard

Snow is swirling all around her. Nothing's alive in this white world but her and the dogs. The wind is the only sound, cold the only sensation. It's as if Libby has traveled to another planet.

The team walks. They can't run. They can't see more than thirty feet ahead. It's like standing on a tennis court and not being able to spot the net.

Libby's eyes are fixed on the trail markers. She doesn't dare lose sight of them. If she does, she may never find the trail again. The dogs wait patiently for her commands—they seem to know how dangerous the situation is. Not even Bugs barks to move ahead.

The snow stings Libby's face. The wind plucks at her eyes. She can't wear her goggles—she'd see even less. To protect her head, she buries it deep in her hood. She peeks out one eye at a time to locate the markers.

When it gets dark, she camps right next to a marker. That way she won't get lost during the night. Bent forward against the wind, she brings each dog a frozen whitefish. She has to push her way to them as if each gust were a heavy door.

The dogs eat quickly. They keep their backs to the wind. Still, by the time they're finished, they're half buried by blowing snow. Libby's not worried—the snow will protect them from the gusts. The dogs go to sleep curled up with their noses under their tails.

Now Libby must find a way to stay warm through the night. Otherwise, she'll freeze to death long before morning.

First she tries to block the wind. She works hard emptying the sled. Then she makes a pile of all her gear along one of its sides. The pile will cut the wind down as she sleeps in the sled.

Her jacket is damp. She's been sweating even in this cold. She's got to get the jacket off or the sweat will soak into her sleeping bag. If that happens, the bag will soon be lined with ice.

The cold is awful. She's afraid to take the jacket off. To make herself think straight, she starts talking out loud. "Take your jacket off," she orders herself. She can't unzip it with her mittens—she must use her bare hands. "Blow on your fingers. Warm them," she quickly commands.

She gets the jacket off and hauls on her pullover parka. By now, though, her fingers are nearly numb. She stuffs them under her pants and spreads them out on her belly. Blood comes throbbing through—that means she doesn't have frostbite.

"You're doing great," Libby comforts herself. She's feeling less frightened now that she's in her warmest clothes. She gets into the sled and slips into her sleeping bag.

The wind is howling. The sled rocks from side to side. But Libby falls asleep, sure she'll make it through the night.

The next thing she knows, the morning light is in her eyes. The wind hasn't let up. The snow is still flying. She doesn't want to move, but she makes herself rise.

She tugs at her sleeping bag. Something's wrong—the zipper won't budge! It has frozen solid. Now the bag is a prison.

Quickly, Libby puts her bare hands over the zipper. Their warmth slowly melts the ice until she can scrape it away. Then she makes her cold, stiff fingers unzip the bag.

Now she can get up. It's freezing in the wind! Standing in her socks, she pulls on her mukluks as fast as possible. Her jacket lies by the sled,

frozen as an iceberg. She has to dig through snowdrifts to find all her gear.

Like a thousand needles, snowflakes prick her face. Suddenly she forgets about the pain—she can't see the dogs! She calls out: "Brownie? Where are you, old boy? Come on, Sister. Dugan? Up you go, Duke." What will she do if the dogs are lost?

Like four-footed snowmen, they slowly rise out of the drifts. They shake off and seem to smile. They're eager to race again.

The team travels slowly. They're on the sea ice now. To move, they have to fight gusts of sixty miles per hour. Often, Libby stops to dust snow off the dogs' faces.

Libby's too nervous to be hungry, but she forces herself to eat. It's the only way to keep her energy level high. With her back to the wind, she drinks some seal oil. Seal oil has a lot of fat. It gives her strength and warmth.

As she eats some chocolate, the dogs gobble down chunks of lamb meat. All at once Libby decides it's time for Sister to take the lead.

As the team plows forward, a rush of wind clears the air. For just an instant, Libby sees colors and shapes in the distance. She brushes snow from her eyes—those are mountains ahead. She can see the frozen sea stretching out till it meets the shore.

Land lies in front of her! Safety is nearby. Sister will take them these few miles and she and the dogs will survive. She hollers and cheers.

The dogs stare at her as though she's gone insane. Then the whiteout quickly closes in again. When the wind rips her cheeks, Libby realizes she might get frostbitten. She's got to find something fast to cover her face. She digs through her gear. All she has are purple dog booties. There's no choice—she stuffs a half dozen of them evenly around her hood. They flap over her face—but they keep it warm. She knows she must be a strange sight, but she doesn't care.

Mile after mile, Libby runs beside the sled. Sometimes she pushes it to help the dogs move faster. But they don't reach land—has Sister gone the wrong way? She's been counting on Sister, and now the old dog has failed her.

Suddenly the markers stop. The trail disappears. Libby has no idea which direction to head in. What now? Could she come this close to victory and still lose the race?

Maybe the mushers were right. Some said this year's Iditarod was jinxed. There have been so many storms, so many delays. This is the thirteenth Iditarod, and thirteen is an unlucky number.

They move onto green ice that's very slippery. Sister pulls to the left, but Libby wants to go right. The stubborn dog won't listen when Libby shouts, "Gee, Sister."

Libby is frightened. Could they be completely lost? She fears Sister's going in the wrong direction, out to the open sea. At any second they'll plunge into icy waves.

Libby screams at Sister. The dog just ignores her. Her ears are back and she trots on as if she knows where she's going.

"You stubborn old rattlesnake," Libby shouts into the wind. "Sister, you airhead, you're going to get us lost." Finally she grows quiet. She can't make Sister obey.

All of a sudden, Libby sees a dark shape ahead. Sister pulls faster. Libby keeps staring in front of her. Through the flying flakes she can make out a trail marker! Sister leads them straight to it. The old dog knew where they were heading all along.

Libby is embarrassed. She stops the sled and goes to Sister. The dog looks right at her as if to say, "I told you so." Libby apologizes—Sister has come through after all. She feels so proud of Sister, and the whole team.

Later she finds that Sister's back legs are frostbitten. Sister never let on—she was too tough for that. She has brought Libby and the team safely through the blizzard—and closer to winning the Iditarod.

Chapter 8

Nome, Sweet Nome

Two days later, Libby's about thirty miles from Nome. Despite two wrong turns, she's held on to her lead. Now she speeds along the beach to the city.

She's tired yet excited. Her dream of winning the Iditarod may really come true. But she's also a little sad. She had to leave Sister at a checkpoint—her frostbite got worse. Libby wanted Sister to be there at the finish line.

Just outside of Nome, some snowmobiles rush toward her. They carry many photographers snapping picture after picture. Overhead a helicopter whirls and buzzes. Television cameras are aboard, filming her victory.

Suddenly Libby hears the screech of a siren. When the first musher approaches Nome, a siren goes off. It's a signal to the city that the race is about to end.

Libby can't stop smiling. She's really going to win the Iditarod. Three thousand people line the streets. They are screaming and shouting.

The team runs along as though they're not the least bit tired. Dusty is afraid of crowds, but the other dogs pull him past. Axle is nervous too—he keeps looking from side to side. But nothing bothers Dugan—he trots ahead proudly.

Libby spots the wooden arch that marks the finish line. As the sled crosses it, her friends rush to greet her. It's official now—she's won the Iditarod! And she's the first woman to ever do it.

Her prize is fifty thousand dollars and a big silver bowl. Dugan and Axle are named the best lead dogs of the race. Libby can't help feeling that Sister should have been there, too.

The crowd keeps roaring. They holler congratulations. As flashbulbs explode, Libby keeps her arms around Dugan and Axle. She has already decided what to do when they all reach home. The team is going to get special treats. There'll be boxes of dog biscuits and thick, tasty steaks. She'll get them piles of fresh straw to lie on, and make sure they take a vacation.

People in the crowd treat her like a real heroine. Libby has shown the mushers that women can do what men do.

But what means the most to her is another award she receives. Libby gets the prize for the musher who takes the best care of her team. She's proud she's cared so well for them. To Libby, her dogs are the true heroes of the race.

Libby grins at the crowd. She beams at the cameras. She's never been so tired in her life—or so happy.

Want to Know More?

Books

Racing Sled Dogs by Michael Cooper (Clarion Books, 1988, 96 pages). All the beginner needs to know about the sport. With photographs.

Black Star, Bright Dawn by Scott O'Dell (Houghton Mifflin, 1988, 144 pages). A story about a girl who must race the Iditarod alone after her father is injured.

When you are older, you might want to read *Race Across Alaska* by Libby Riddles and Tim Jones (Stackpole, 1988, 239 pages). In her own words, Libby tells how she won the grueling race.

Visit

You can visit Alaska during the Iditarod. Lots of spectators go to Anchorage for the start of the race and to Nome for the finish. During the race (but a few days behind the mushers), there is even a tour of the Iditarod trail led by a former musher! For more information, write Joe Reddington, Sr., H.C. 30 Box 5460, Wasilla, Alaska 99654.

Want to Be a Musher?

If you're at least fourteen years old, you can race in an Iditarod—a special one called the Junior Iditarod. It was set up in 1977 by some Alaska teenagers who wanted the chance to race their dogs.

The 130-mile Junior Iditarod is run each year in February. To enter, you must be between the ages of fourteen and seventeen. (Eighteen-year-olds can run in the Iditarod Trail Sled Dog Race.)

Junior Iditarod contestants have to practice

very hard. They usually have their own dog teams that they've known and trained for years. Many junior mushers go on to enter the longer race.

If you want more information on the Junior Iditarod, write to the Iditarod Trail Committee.

The Iditarod Trail Committee

An organization called the Iditarod Trail Committee is in charge of both the Iditarod Trail Sled Dog Race and the Junior Iditarod. It draws up the rules for the races.

The committee is also a great source of information on the races. It sells books, videos, and special products (like mugs and T-shirts) through the mail. It also sends out school information packets that are full of facts, games, and puzzles.

You can write the Iditarod Trail Committee at P.O. Box 870800, Wasilla, Alaska 99687, or call 1-800-545-6874.

Glossary

booties special soft socks to protect a dog's paws from cold and ice. Usually handsewn by each musher, they must be completely free of holes and fit snugly but not too tightly.

checkpoint a required stop where the musher and team can rest, eat, and change equipment. Race officials examine the sleds and make sure each musher signs in. A veterinarian looks over the dogs. A checkpoint may be a town or just a cabin or camp.

dehydration the loss of too much water from the body. Dehydration can make people and dogs sick.

frostbite this happens when extreme cold injures any part of the body. Fingers and toes are often affected.

"Gee!" the musher's command to the team to turn right.

hallucination seeing or hearing something that isn't really there. Mushers sometimes hallucinate when they're extremely tired.

harness a system of straps that sled dogs wear around their bodies when pulling a sled. A rope called the *tug line* connects the harness to the *tow line*, or main rope, which is attached to the sled.

"Haw!" the musher's command to the team to turn left.

hypothermia this happens when a person gets so cold his or her body temperature falls below normal. Hypothermia causes muscle weakness, fatigue, and fuzzy thinking. Eventually, the heart and lungs stop working. People can die from hypothermia.

kamamik an Eskimo ice cream made of reindeer fat, seal oil, salmonberries, and sugar.

lead dog the dog at the head of the team. The

other dogs follow the lead dog.

mukluks especially warm, soft boots made of seal or reindeer skin and lined with fur. They were developed by Eskimos.

"Mush!" the musher's command to the team to get going. It comes from the French word *marchons*, or "let's go!"

musher a dog sled driver or racer.

northern lights ribbons, streaks, and clouds of colored lights that appear in the night skies of the Far North. Also called the aurora borealis.

swing dog the dog right behind the lead dog. The swing dog helps steer the sled.

tow line the main rope that runs from the sled. Each dog is connected to it by a *tug line*. The tow line is also called the gang line.

tug line a rope that connects the dog's harness to the main rope, or *tow line*.

tundra a region in very cold climates, such as Alaska, that is flat and treeless.

wheel dog the last dog of the team and the one closest to the sled.

whiteout this happens when a heavy snowstorm and a very strong wind make it impossible to see anything around you.

"Whoa!" the musher's command to the team to stop.

Index